VIRUSES

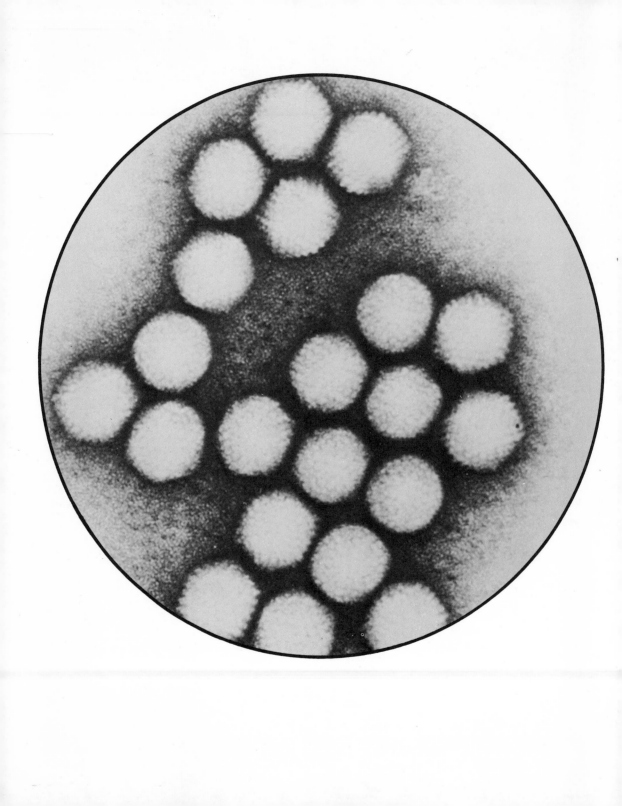

VIRUSES
BY ALAN E. NOURSE, M.D.

A GROLIER COMPANY

FRANKLIN WATTS
NEW YORK | LONDON | TORONTO | SYDNEY | 1983
A FIRST BOOK | REVISED EDITION

Frontis: the adenovirus, one of more than three hundred
kinds of viruses, attacks the mucus-secreting glands in
the respiratory tract and lymph nodes throughout the body.

Photographs courtesy of the Center for Disease Con-
trol: opp. title page, pp. 19 (both), 32, 42, and 46;
The Free Library of Philadelphia: p. 3; The New York
Public Library Picture Collection: pp. 4 and 45; Pfizer,
Inc.: p. 13; WHO: p. 22 (photo by T. Farkas); Taurus
Photos: p. 39 (top left, ® Gary W. Grimes; top right
and bottom by Martin M. Rotker); n.c.: p. 46; Ameri-
can Cancer Society: pp. 50 (both) and 54 (both).

Diagrams by Vantage Art, Inc.

Library of Congress Cataloging in Publication Data

Nourse, Alan Edward.
    Viruses.

    A revised edition.
    (A First book)
    Bibliography: p.
    Includes Index.
    Summary: Describes the complexity of viruses,
the difficulty of isolating them, common
and uncommon viral diseases, vaccines and
immunity, and modern virus research.
    1. Viruses—Juvenile Literature.   [1. Viruses]
I. Title.
QR365.N68 1983   616'.0194   82-16010
ISBN 0-531-04534-X

CONTENTS

THE ENIGMATIC VIRUSES

One day in 1796 in a little town in Gloucestershire, England, an obscure country doctor put his professional reputation—and the life of a young patient—in jeopardy by undertaking a startling and dangerous experiment. First, the doctor made two small incisions on the arm of his patient, a healthy eight-year-old boy named James Phipps. Next, he took infected matter from a sore on a local milkmaid's hand and rubbed it into the wound. As everyone expected, the boy soon developed a sore there just like the milkmaid's—a minor infection that soon healed.

But six weeks later a second and more dangerous step was taken. This time the doctor took infected matter from a victim of smallpox, one of the most dreaded and deadly diseases of the day, and rubbed it into Master Phipps' arm. By all accounts, the boy should have been overcome by smallpox within a few days, but this time it didn't happen. The physician, Edward Jenner, became famous the world over for discovering a safe and sure means of preventing a terrible epidemic disease, and the boy remained safe from smallpox for the rest of his life.

Jenner's discovery was almost an accident. In his day, practically everbody got smallpox sooner or later. Some 30 percent died from the disease, and many who survived were permanently disfigured by the ugly pockmark scars the infection left behind. Nobody knew what caused the disease, but Jenner had heard an old folktale that milkmaids who contracted cowpox, a minor infection that caused a few quickly healing sores on the hands, would never catch smallpox. The more Jenner considered this, the more he wondered if it might be true. Perhaps he tried his technique first on members of his own family—nobody knows for sure—but at last he became so certain it would work that he was willing to try his historic experiment on young Master Phipps.

Jenner called his technique "vaccination," from *vaccinia*, the Latin name for cowpox. His success brought him honor and fame throughout the Western world.

In spite of this success, Jenner had no idea what *caused* smallpox. Nor did' Louis Pasteur, almost ninety years later, know what caused rabies on the day that young Joseph Meister was brought to his laboratory, badly bitten by a rabid dog. He did know that rabies was transmitted to humans from the bite of an infected dog or other animal and that the disease was invariably fatal once the first symp-

In 1796, Dr. Edward Jenner undertook a dangerous experiment when he "vaccinated" a young boy against smallpox by deliberately infecting him with a minor cowpox virus several weeks before introducing smallpox into the boy's system.

toms occurred, dooming the victim to a horrible and painful death. He also knew that certain kinds of infections were caused by tiny organisms known as bacteria, and he thought perhaps rabies was, too. What was more, he had found that by transferring bits of infected nervous tissue from one laboratory dog to another, the infected tissue's power to cause fatal rabies seemed to grow weaker and weaker.

It was an extract made from just such "weakened" infective material that Pasteur used as a vaccine in the hope of protecting young Joseph Meister from the dreaded disease even after he had been bitten. And as week followed week, the boy remained free of rabies. Pasteur's antirabies vaccine was effective, even though he had no way of knowing that the cause of the disease was, in fact, a virus—an infective agent so very tiny that it could not be seen even with the aid of the microscopes available at the time.

AN ANCIENT FOE

Today we think of Jenner and Pasteur as pioneers in battling a silent and invisible foe that they could neither understand nor observe. But humankind had been suffering from viral-borne epidemics since long before recorded history. The so-called Great Red Plague that Thucydides described in his account of the ancient war between Athens and Sparta may have been nothing more than a terrible epidemic of

Louis Pasteur successfully used infectious rabies material to treat a young boy who had been bitten by a rabid dog.

●5

rubeola, or red measles, still a familiar viral infection today. The mummified remains of ancient Egyptian pharaohs and their families have shown deformities characteristic of paralytic poliomyelitis, another dreaded viral disease.

Smallpox, so called to distinguish it from the "Great Pox," a name used for syphilis, was widespread in Europe during the Middle Ages. When American soldiers and pioneers moved across the Great Plains in the early 1800s, the smallpox they brought with them took more Indian lives than all the Indian wars put together. Yellow fever, still another viral disease, struck repeatedly in the eastern coastal cities of America in the late 1700s, culminating in a fearful epidemic in the city of Philadelphia in 1793. More recently, the worldwide epidemic of influenza during 1918 and 1919 afflicted as many as *half a billion* people and contributed to the deaths of some ten million, many of whom succumbed to pneumonia and other bacterial infections on the heels of the flu virus. What is more, we now know that viruses are responsible for diseases ranging from head colds and fever blisters to infectious hepatitis, and they are now known to be the cause of many childhood afflictions such as chicken pox, rubella ("German measles"), and mumps.

For all this long acquaintance with viral infections, it has been within only the past fifty years that medical researchers have really begun to understand exactly what viruses are, how they behave, and—above all—how they invade living tissues to cause such a multitude of diseases. But today, thanks to great leaps in the field of microbiology, scientists have not only tracked down many of the major disease-causing viruses. They have also, in the process, learned much about the riddle of heredity—the way in which the physical characteristics of cells and tissues are handed down from one generation to the next—and may even discover some of the secrets of life itself.

THE ELUSIVE INVADERS

Why did viruses remain shrouded in mystery for so long? As early as the mid-1600s, scientists were becoming aware that the world is populated with multitudes of tiny organisms, so very small they can be seen only with the aid of a microscope. Two hundred years later, Louis Pasteur proved for the first time that certain of these tiny organisms, by then known as *bacteria,* are the cause of certain infectious diseases. Between 1850 and 1900 many different kinds of infectious bacteria were identified. The tuberculosis bacterium, the streptococcus organism that causes scarlet fever, and the staphylococci responsible for pimples and boils were all discovered. Still smaller microbes, the rickettsia, were found to cause typhus fever and Rocky Mountain spotted fever. All these tiny organisms could be seen under the microscope with special staining techniques and would grow and reproduce when placed in a special nutrient broth or spread on a gelatinlike substance known as agar.

But viruses were something else. These entities, whatever they were, proved to be so incredibly tiny that the most powerful of all light microscopes could not detect them. While small bacteria such as the streptococci are approximately one micron in diameter (that is, about 4/100,000 of an inch), the very largest viruses known today are only about one third that size, and many viruses are as much as thirty-five times smaller, some less than *one millionth* of an inch in diameter—smaller than some individual protein molecules!

Indeed, early researchers were able to identify viruses at all only because they could be made to pass through filters containing holes so small that the comparatively large bacteria were held back. Even today, most viruses can be observed only by using electron microscopes, which are capable of magnifying their images anywhere from 40,000 to 100,000 times.

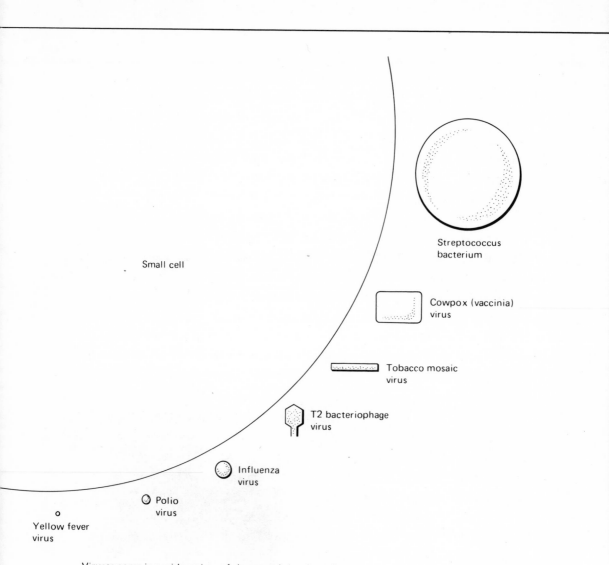

Small cell

Streptococcus
bacterium

Cowpox (vaccinia)
virus

Tobacco mosaic
virus

T2 bacteriophage
virus

Influenza
virus

Polio
virus

Yellow fever
virus

Viruses come in a wide variety of shapes and sizes but all are smaller than the tiniest known bacteria

Tiny as they are, viruses come in a wide variety of sizes and shapes. Some appear fluffy, like cotton balls; others are like long, thin rods. Still others look like many-sided crystals. One type of virus resembles a six-sided bullet, while another looks like a rolling pin with one handle missing.

All told, more than three hundred kinds of viruses are now known to invade the human body, some transmitted in the air, others carried in droplets of moisture from the sneezes and coughing of infected persons, still others carried in food or water that has been contaminated by infected human waste. Hundreds of other viruses, harmless to people, attack other life forms. Cats and dogs, for instance, can be infected by distemper viruses or parvoviruses, which leave human beings unharmed. We know that viruses can enter our bodies through virtually any mucous membrane—through the respiratory tract, for instance, or the intestine, or the lining of the eyes—and can cause well over fifty different kinds of human disease. And while some viruses seem harmless to humans or cause only nuisance-type infections, not a single one yet has been found to be helpful in any way, in contrast to the many bacteria that perform useful tasks within the body.

DEAD OR ALIVE?

The early virus-hunters assumed that viruses were merely very tiny bacteria—that they lived independent lives of their own; reproduced themselves as bacteria do, by cellular division; and were capable of growth, movement, energy production, and all the other life functions of bacteria. But little by little it became painfully clear that not one of these assumptions was true. The more we studied viruses the more we realized that they are, in fact, a totally different kind of entity than any of the bacteria.

•9

For one thing, all the viruses known today are totally parasitic. They can live and reproduce only inside the living cells of some susceptible host—for instance, in the lung of a mouse, in the cells of a chick embryo still growing in its shell, or in the cells of the respiratory tract, liver, or intestine of a human. Isolated from living cells, viruses are as lifeless as sawdust. They can do nothing for themselves but sit and wait for a host to come along.

Does this mean that viruses outside of a living host are "dead"? Even today scientists hedge on this question. We know that the viruses' power to infect living cells can be destroyed by intense heat, by contact with certain germicidal solutions or solvents, and by radiation. Otherwise, however, viruses are remarkably hardy. They do not "die," as do many bacteria, when deprived of nutrients or water. They can remain in their inert but potentially dangerous state of "half-life" for months or years, possibly for centuries. Even freezing does not seem to bother them. There may well be inactive viruses surviving on specks of dust in outer space, totally unharmed or unchanged, for ages on end. What is more, only a few viruses are affected by antibioticlike drugs that can destroy so many of the disease-causing bacteria.

The truth is that viruses are not really living cells at all, by any ordinary definition. They contain no protoplasm, the semifluid life substance that fills most living cells. They have no cell membranes surrounding them, as normal cells do, nor can they, by themselves, use the simple sugars, fats, and amino acids that living cells utilize to produce energy or build protein. Among other things, this means that viruses cannot grow. Some are so completely unlifelike that they can actually be crystallized in pure form in the laboratory, as lifeless and harmless as salt in a shaker—until they come in contact with susceptible living cells.

For all these shortcomings, however, viruses possess one power that sets them far apart from any other disease-causing microbe. Though unable themselves to perform any of the vital life functions of which even the lowliest bacteria are capable, viruses do have the amazing capacity *to force the living cells of their hosts to perform those life functions for them.* And herein lies the viruses' "secret of life" and their deadly danger as well.

NATURE'S TINIEST TYRANTS

If they really are not "exceedingly tiny bacteria," then what exactly *are* these tiny parasites, and how can they force the living cells in the bodies of their hosts to obey their commands? Essentially, viruses are nothing more than molecule-size packets of nucleic acid, a complex organic compound, surrounded by protective coatings of protein.

Today we know that nucleic acids in one form or another make up the remarkable genetic material found in the nuclei of all living cells. It is these nucleic acids that make it possible for cells to reproduce themselves and to pass on their own individual characteristics to new generations of cells. Viruses are really little more than tiny bundles of this hereditary material without the living matter around them. They are sometimes described as "chromosomes on the loose," tiny packets of "infectious heredity," and it is their nucleic acid that is the key to their power.

Within the nucleus of a living cell, molecules of the nucleic acid known as DNA (short for "deoxyribonucleic acid") act as the "master molecules," controlling the cell's many vital life functions. These molecules ensure faithful duplication of the cell when it reproduces by cell division, and they direct a similar nucleic acid known as RNA (for "ribonucleic acid") in the cell's manufacture of vital proteins and enzymes. But when a susceptible cell is attacked by a virus, the DNA or RNA from the virus, very similar to that of the cell itself, pours into the cell and sets up a new "master control system" all its own, with a totally different purpose. Instead of directing the manufacture of substances useful to the cell, the viral nucleic acid takes over the cell's entire chemical system and forces it to produce enough viral nucleic acid molecules and protein coatings to form hundreds or even thousands of new, fully formed virus particles.

This whole process can proceed with breathtaking swiftness. In some cases as little as twenty-four minutes may elapse from the instant the virus particle first attaches itself to the outside of its cell victim until the cell bursts apart to release the hundreds of new virus particles that have been formed within it. Then, with the host cell drained and depleted, perhaps even destroyed, each of the newly formed virus particles goes forth to attack another cell, and the whole process is repeated again and again, leaving an ever expanding trail of dead or damaged host cells behind.

PATTERNS OF INFECTION

Other viruses are more subtle. In some cases, for example, the virus particles attach their nucleic acid to the DNA molecules in the host-cell nucleus and then, in effect, "hide out" for prolonged periods of time. Rather than forcing immediate replication of the virus particles, the viral nucleic acid remains attached to the host-cell DNA and is reproduced each time the host cell is reproduced. As a result, several generations of host cells may be silently infected by the original virus particle. Then later, when conditions are right, the viral nucleic acid can become active in all the affected cells at once, releasing tens of thousands of new virus particles in a single wave!

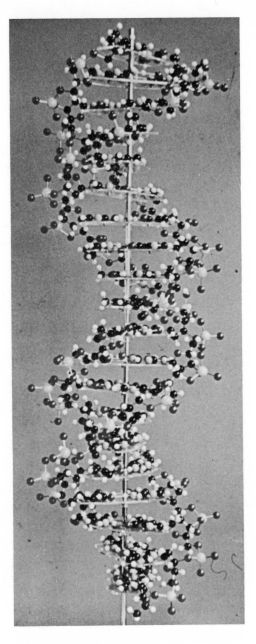

A model showing the
molecular structure of
deoxyribonucleic acid (DNA).
Viruses do their damage by
entering the body's cells
and replacing normal DNA
with viral nucleic acid.

Obviously a viral attack can cause enormous damage to the host in a surprisingly short time. If lung tissues are attacked, the victim may develop a widespread viral pneumonia within a very few days. If the virus affects the spinal cord, paralysis or even death may quickly occur as the nerve cells controlling muscular movements or breathing movements are permanently destroyed. If liver cells are involved, the victim may die quite suddenly of liver failure. Even when the invaders cause no immediate symptoms or damage at all, they may still remain lodged within their host cells for months or even years, just waiting to do their damage some time in the future when conditions are right.

Fortunately, our bodies are not entirely helpless against these deadly destroyers. Viruses have one critical characteristic that works against them. The protective protein coatings, different from any protein material normally found in our bodies, can stimulate the formation of special protective substances in our bloodstreams to help fight off the viral attackers. These substances, known as antibodies, can block the entrance of newly formed virus particles into new host cells. Thus, they can gradually slow down and terminate the production of new virus particles.

But time is required for an effective army of protective antibodies to be manufactured. Meanwhile, the viral invasion proceeds at full speed, causing damage and destruction to body tissues as it goes. It was in search of ways to help speed up the body's natural defenses against viral diseases—perhaps even prevent the viral invasion altogether—that the first serious study of viruses was begun.

2
TRACKING DOWN THE VIRAL INVADERS

During the closing years of the last century, microbe-hunters faced a perplexing problem in identifying the microbes responsible for certain common and dangerous infective diseases. How could you track down an enemy that you could neither see nor understand, an entity so tiny and elusive that you could not even be sure that it existed at all?

Today the field of virology—the study of the nature and behavior of viruses—is one of the most fascinating and exciting of all fields of medical research. We are familiar with the names of such modern virus-hunters as Jonas Salk and Albert Sabin, the men who pioneered the vaccines that protect us today from the ravages of poliomyelitis. Almost every day we see news reports of the research going on in modern virus laboratories. It is hard to believe that as little as seventy-five years ago medical scientists were not entirely certain that viruses even existed. Even after these tiny tyrants had finally been discovered and identified, it took decades of tedious laboratory work to learn what they really were and how they might be conquered. In those days there were no famous names in virus research, no exciting breakthroughs. But scientists stubbornly per-

•15

sisted, piecing together the groundwork that finally led to an explosion of discovery in virus laboratories all over the world during the past thirty years.

THE EARLIEST CLUES

Why was the early study of viruses so difficult? For one thing, researchers did not know what they were looking for. By the late 1800s, researchers knew that certain bacteria were responsible for many infectious diseases. Single-celled animallike organisms called protozoa caused other infections, while even tinier microorganisms known as rickettsia brought about still others. Soon, the early microbe-hunters were convinced that *all* infectious diseases might be traced to specific microorganisms, if only the right ones could be found.

Yet the microbes that caused certain of humankind's worst infectious diseases—smallpox, rabies, and yellow fever, to name a few—continued to evade discovery. Brilliant scientists searched in vain, and then, when a breakthrough finally came in 1892, hardly anyone even noticed it.

The person responsible was an obscure Russian researcher named Dmitri Ivanovski, and he was not studying human diseases at all. His concern was a plant disease that caused mottling and destruction of tobacco leaves. Searching for the bacteria that might be responsible, Ivanovski crushed the infected leaves in sterile water and then passed the water through an earthenware filter with pores so tiny that even the smallest known bacteria would be trapped. To his chagrin, however, the infective agent he was seeking seemed to pass right through; the clear, filtered solution still retained its power to infect tobacco leaves even after it had been filtered again and again.

Ivanovski published a report of his odd findings, but it received little notice. Then, six years later, in 1898, the same experiments were done independently by a Dutch botanist named Martinus Willem Beijerinck. Like Ivanovski, Beijerinck found that the infective agent, whatever its nature, could infect healthy tobacco plants even after many filtrations but that it could easily be destroyed by heating the filtrate. Convinced that he had discovered some totally new disease-producing agent that existed in a fluid state, he called it a *contagium vivum fluidum*—a "contagious living fluid." Later he applied the name *virus* to his discovery, from a Latin word meaning "poison."

Soon, other investigators began discovering similar "filterable" disease agents. In 1898, Friedrich Loeffler and Paul Frosch proved that hoof-and-mouth disease, an extremely contagious infection of cattle, was caused by such an agent. In 1901, Walter Reed and a team of American scientists showed that yellow fever was also transmitted by such a "contagious fluid." Then, as dozens of other diseases were traced to these strange, elusive entities, they became known as "filterable viruses."

For all this flurry of discovery, however, the early virus-hunters knew virtually nothing about these filterable infective agents. There seemed to be no way to study them directly the way disease-producing bacteria had been studied. Except for one or two so-called great viruses, which could be seen as hazy blobs at the very outer limit of microscopic magnification, most of the newly discovered viruses simply could not be seen at all; they appeared to be far smaller than even the smallest bacteria known. Nor could any of them be made to grow or reproduce in the kinds of nutrient broths in which bacteria flourished. Indeed, it seemed to be necessary to devise a whole series of new laboratory techniques in order to learn anything at all about the elusive quarry.

●17

THE TOOLS FOR
VIRUS-HUNTING

As a first step, investigators began refining and improving their filters to help distinguish one virus from another. In 1931, an American scientist named W. J. Elford tried using filters made from collodion, a porous, plasticlike material that had previously been used for coating wounds. Elford devised a series of collodion membranes with pores of known, graded sizes to sort out viruses. He soon demonstrated that each of a number of known viruses had its own characteristic size. Some, such as the vaccinia virus, causing cowpox, were comparatively huge, almost as large as the tiniest known bacteria. Others were only one tenth or one twentieth the size of the vaccinia virus, while still others were so much smaller that they could easily pass through the finest filters Elford could create.

About the same time it was found that the ordinary laboratory centrifuge could be used to differentiate viruses. Each virus seemed to have its own characteristic weight as well as size, so the heavier viruses sank to the bottom of the centrifuge tube faster than the lighter ones. The virus of influenza was first identified by this method. So also was a virus that came to be known as T2, later used in many virus experiments. But unfortunately, such techniques told investigators very little except that all viruses were very small and were type-specific, meaning simply that a given virus of identifiable size and weight always caused the same disease.

Then, in the early 1930s, virus-hunters turned to chemical analysis to learn more about the makeup and behavior of individual viruses. Wendell M. Stanley, an American biochemist, began studying the tobacco mosaic virus to find out what it was made of. First he froze infected tobacco leaves in order to rupture the

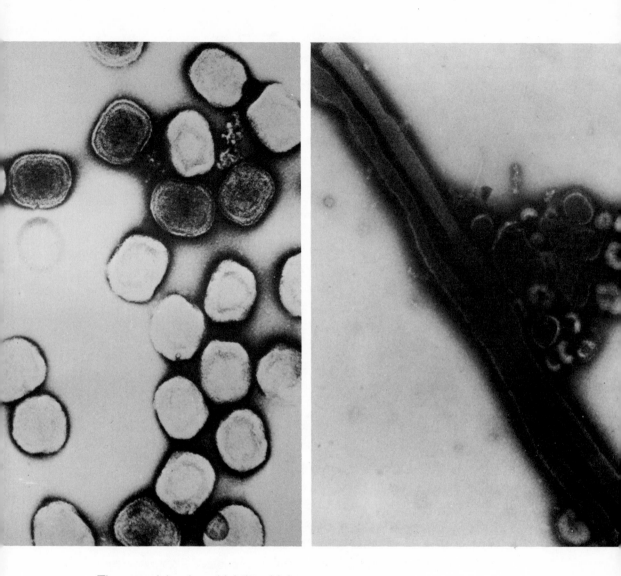

The vaccinia virus (right), which causes cowpox, is almost as large as tiny bacteria; the influenza virus (left), though similar in shape, is much smaller.

infected cells. Then he ground the leaves into chemical solutions for filtration. The filtrates, containing the virus and a number of plant protein materials as well, were then further treated in order to isolate the virus in purified form. Finally, the virus itself was subjected to chemical analysis to determine its characteristic chemical components. Other workers carried out similar assaults on other viruses, and over the years this tedious, unromantic work began to pay off.

It was found, for example, that all viruses seemed to contain two kinds of biochemical constituents—nucleic acids and proteins. Beyond this, however, viruses seemed to differ widely one from another. Some seemed ridiculously simple, consisting of a single tiny bundle of nucleic acid surrounded by a protein coating—and nothing more. Others, especially the larger viruses, had more complex chemical structures, including carbohydrate molecules, fatty material, copper or sodium salts, enzymes, sometimes even vitamins, together with their basic proteins and nucleic acids. These complex viruses seemed far more like ordinary bacteria than their tinier, simpler cousins, but researchers still argued whether they were truly living organisms or merely complex chemical poisons.

Then, about 1940, the use of a special kind of microscope opened a whole new wave of virus research and caused scientists to take a new and different look at the question of viral "life." Ordinary light microscopes failed to reveal viruses for a very simple reason—most were considerably smaller than the average wavelength of light. Bacteria could be seen under such microscopes because light passing through would strike them and cast a shadow that could be focused into a sharp image. But viruses were so tiny that they could, in effect, "hide" between the wavelengths. What was needed was a microscope using some form of "light" with a much shorter wavelength than visible light. Someone eventually thought of using a stream of electrons—tiny negatively charged elementary particles that possess marked wavelike qualities—instead of visible light, and the electron microscope was invented.

This device worked very much like an ordinary light microscope with a few key modifications. Instead of a beam of light, a beam of electrons was sent through a long hollow tube to strike a sample of virus-containing material. Electrons striking this sample were scattered every which way, but the unscattered electrons could be focused, by means of electromagnets, onto a fluorescent screen at the end of the tube. And there, like magic, clear images of the long-sought-after virus particles could be seen. Later investigators found that by coating the specimen with a layer of vaporized gold just before the examination, the image on the screen could be markedly intensified, with the viruses appearing in sharp, three-dimensional relief, magnified between 40,000 and 100,000 times.

THE QUARRY TRAPPED

With the help of the electron microscope, virus research in the 1930s and 1940s at last began to make real progress. With clear photographs showing viruses of many shapes and sizes, there could no longer be any doubt that these elusive entities indeed existed.

But living organisms? More and more of the evidence suggested that they might be. For one thing, they *could* reproduce, which even the most complex organic chemicals known could not do. True, they could only manage this with the aid (and at the expense) of other living cells, but during the 1930s virus-workers found ways to study virus reproduction in the laboratory. Research-

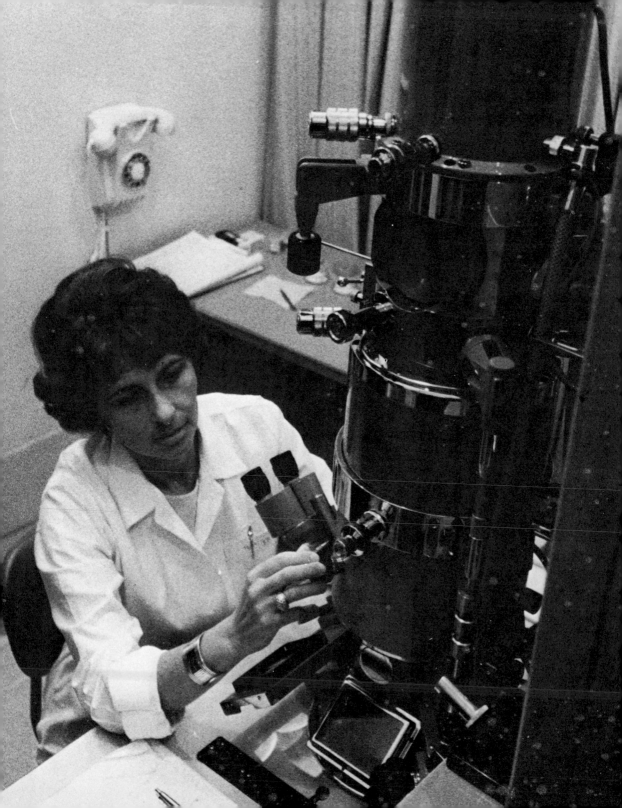

ers such as Alice M. Woodruff and Ernest W. Goodpasture, for example, lifted sections of eggshell away from living chick embryos and inoculated the embryos with a variety of viruses, which then multiplied rapidly in this living culture medium—a technique still used today in manufacturing certain kinds of virus vaccines.

Such experiments revealed interesting things about virus behavior. Many viruses, for instance, underwent significant changes when transferred from one living tissue culture to another. Some of them seemed to mutate, or change, into quite different viruses with different properties after a succession of such transfers. In the process, a number of them seemed to gradually lose their disease-producing potential, becoming progressively less virulent. This later proved to be extremely important; by using certain dangerous strains of viruses that had become weakened, or *attenuated* (from a Latin word meaning "diluted" or "made thin"), it was sometimes possible to develop vaccines that could protect people from infection by the more virulent, unweakened strains of the viruses. Thus, a vaccine against dengue fever, a severe influenzalike infection of the tropics, was made by attenuating certain strains of virulent dengue fever viruses. Likewise, the Sabin polio vaccines and some early measles vaccines were made from attenuated viruses.

The invention of the electron microscope enabled scientists to clearly view viruses for the first time.

Unfortunately, however, the ability of certain viruses to mutate into different forms led to problems as well as advantages. It was found, for example, that the viruses that cause influenza could mutate so frequently and so completely that vaccines made to protect against the older strains had little protective effect against new forms that were constantly appearing. Even today we still have worldwide epidemics of "new" forms of flu, such as the Russian flu virus that appeared in 1978, attacking mostly young people, or the recent A/Texas and A/Victoria strains infecting Americans of all ages.

From the beginning, virus research has been time-consuming and tedious, but with the aid of electron microscopy and tissue-culturing techniques, virologists have learned more and more about the nature and behavior of many viruses. At the same time, they have learned more about a number of viral diseases, some minor, some deadly, that have plagued humankind since before recorded history and that continue to plague us today.

3
COMMON AND UNCOMMON VIRAL DISEASES

It happens to everyone at one time or another. You wake up with a scratchy throat and a headache, and by evening you have a fever, aching muscles, a stuffy nose, and a cough. Next morning you feel even worse. When you finally feel sick enough to see your doctor, he or she examines you and says, "Hard to say, but it's probably some kind of virus. . . ."

Such news may be small comfort, but chances are the doctor is exactly right. Your illness is probably caused by some kind of virus, and beyond that there is nothing much that can be said. Viral infections are almost everyday occurrences in our lives. Over fifty different varieties are recognized today. Common colds may be caused by any of dozens of different so-called rhinoviruses. A wide variety of influenzalike illnesses and respiratory infections, some mild, some severe, are caused by large families of parainfluenza viruses and adenoviruses, distinguishable one from another only in a modern virus laboratory. In fact, there are so many minor viral respiratory or intestinal infections and they occur so often and with such vague symptoms that we don't even try to distinguish them as separate diseases at all. Indeed, we may well live with a long succession of

●25

unidentified minor viral infections from the time we are born until the time we die, many of them causing no more than a few hours of mild discomfort, if that.

A number of viral diseases, however, are not so vague or mysterious at all. Some have very clear, specific, recognizable signs and symptoms. Far from being mild offenders, some of these can cause severe and prolonged illnesses, and a few are outright killers. But mild or dangerous, most viral infections share certain characteristics in common because of the similarities between the viruses that cause them.

GENERAL PATTERNS
OF VIRAL INFECTION

First, viruses are characteristically spread either by way of respiratory tract secretions or through contact with intestinal wastes, and they gain entry into our bodies through mucous membranes. Among those spread by way of coughing, sneezing, kissing, or just close contact in the same room are the families of rhinoviruses and parainfluenza viruses that cause the common cold, influenza, viral bronchitis, and viral pneumonia; and the adenoviruses that attack mucus-secreting glands in the respiratory tract or become lodged in the lymph nodes scattered throughout the body. Another large group, the so-called enteroviruses, attack the cells and organs of the intestinal tract and are spread by direct or indirect contact with infected people, contaminated food or water, or unwashed hands. These viruses are responsible for headaches, fever, and many cases of "summer diarrhea," or gastroenteritis ("intestinal flu"), as well as certain kinds of meningitis. Among the most dangerous of the enteroviruses, strange to say, are those that cause poliomyelitis. Although we do not ordinarily think of polio as an intestinal infection,

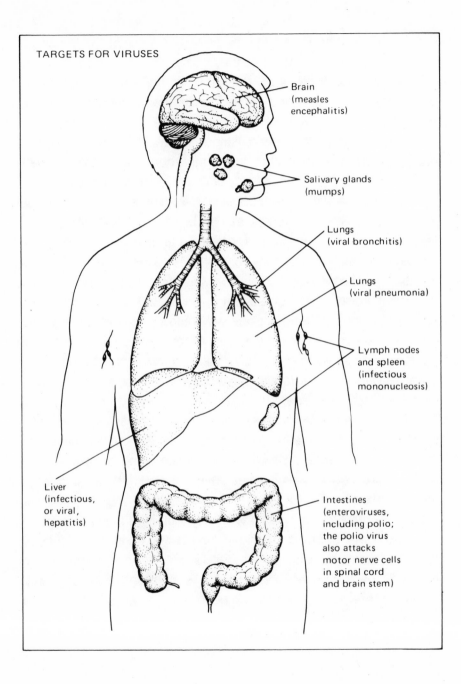

TARGETS FOR VIRUSES

Brain
(measles
encephalitis)

Salivary glands
(mumps)

Lungs
(viral bronchitis)

Lungs
(viral pneumonia)

Lymph nodes
and spleen
(infectious
mononucleosis)

Liver
(infectious,
or viral,
hepatitis)

Intestines
(enteroviruses,
including polio;
the polio virus
also attacks
motor nerve cells
in spinal cord
and brain stem)

in areas where the disease is still prevalent most of the cases go unrecognized as polio because they show symptoms only of a mild diarrheal disease. Only rarely does the virus go on to attack nerve cells in the spinal cord and cause the dreaded symptoms of paralytic polio.

This brings up a second curious characteristic of many disease-producing viruses, that even the most dangerous do not always produce the same severity of illness in one victim as in another. Perhaps one victim may have a partial immunity from a previous attack, or possibly the virus itself has been altered and made less virulent toward the end of an epidemic. In addition, a person's general level of health and vitality may help him or her to resist a viral infection. Among the best ways to avoid serious viral infections are immunization, avoiding contact with an infected person, the maintaining of a strong, healthy body with nutritious meals, and getting plenty of exercise and adequate rest. All too often it is the run-down, exhausted, or malnourished individuals, the very young, the elderly, or those with their resistance lowered by other, unrelated infections who fall victim most easily to viral invaders.

Finally, whether mild or severe, viral infections are often accompanied by certain characteristic signs and symptoms that differ markedly from bacterial infections. The white blood count in a bacterial infection often rises dramatically; in a viral infection it is more likely to fall *below* normal. A low fever of 100° or 101° F (37.8° or 38.3°C) is more common with viral infections than the high fever so often seen with bacterial infections. Headache, nausea, and loss of appetite commonly accompany a viral infection, and the muscles of the back, neck, and legs tend to ache, sometimes so severely that the victim feels as if he or she had been hit by a car or fallen down a flight of stairs.

These symptoms, together with a sense of inordinate tiredness or exhaustion, make up what is known as general malaise (literally, "general ill comfort"), a condition that is so very characteristic of viral infections that doctors can often identify the problem even when no more specific symptoms are present. And indeed, many viral infections tend to leave the victim exhausted and spent for days or weeks—sometimes even months—after the active infection and its symptoms have subsided. This "recovery phase" following certain viral infections can present special dangers because at such times the victim may be highly vulnerable to bacterial infections that appear in the wake of a viral infection.

A CHECKLIST OF VIRAL INFECTIONS

In addition to such general symptoms, many viral infections cause *specific* symptoms related directly to the part of the body that is being attacked. The common cold, for example, causes a runny or plugged-up nose, a scratchy throat, and a tendency to sneeze and cough. In viral bronchitis a dry, hacking cough is commonplace, while the victim of viral pneumonia may suffer pain and tightness in the chest, persistent deep coughing, and sometimes even shortness of breath. Nausea, vomiting, abdominal cramps, and diarrhea often characterize an enterovirus infection. In certain viral infections, a characteristic skin rash may appear. Thus rubeola (red measles) is marked by the appearance of coarse, reddish-brown spots on the skin, while rubella ("German," or "three-day," measles) causes a finer, pinkish-red skin rash. Chicken pox, perhaps the single most contagious infectious disease known, is easily recognized by the tiny watery blisters that appear on the skin all over the body.

Certain other serious viral infections deserve special mention. Among the most troublesome are hepatitis A (also called infectious hepatitis or viral hepatitis), spread by contaminated food or water, and its equally dangerous twin, hepatitis B, or serum hepatitis, commonly transmitted by the use of unsterile hypodermic syringes or by transfusions of contaminated blood. These closely related viruses, plus a third known as hepatitis Non-A, Non-B, all attack and destroy cells in the liver. Along with nausea and fever, there is severe pain in the upper right corner of the abdomen, just under the ribs. As liver cells are destroyed, the bile that is normally released into the digestive tract backs up into the bloodstream instead and causes the skin and the whites of the eyes to turn yellow, a condition known as jaundice. Hepatitis is especially dangerous because the ruined liver cells may not be properly replaced during the healing process, so that permanent liver damage or even death may result.

Crowded housing and poor sanitation have led to serious epidemics of hepatitis A and hepatitis Non-A, Non-B in some of our major cities during late summer and fall. Fortunately, those who have been exposed can obtain temporary protection by the use of gamma globulin, a portion of the blood serum that contains protective antibodies and can prevent the virus from gaining a foothold if it is used early enough after infection. And in 1981 an effective vaccine against hepatitis B was finally perfected and received approval from the U.S. Food and Drug Administration (FDA).

A FAMILY OF VILLAINS

Another common—and often very puzzling—viral infection goes by the jawbreaking name of infectious mononucleosis, so called because of a certain kind of white blood cell that appears in the bloodstream in its presence. For most victims, "infectious mono" is a comparatively mild disease, but its symptoms may linger for weeks—longer than most viral diseases—and some victims are disabled for months with swollen lymph glands, fever, exhaustion, intermittent skin rashes, and swelling of the liver and spleen. Adolescents and young adults seem most prone to the infection, and today's evidence suggests that the offending virus is transmitted in the saliva, accounting for the nickname "kissing disease." No vaccine exists to prevent it, but even a mild case confers lasting immunity.

Today we know that infectious mononucleosis is caused by the so-called Epstein-Barr virus, discovered in 1964 by British virologists M. S. Epstein and Y. M. Barr. This virus is one of a group of notorious troublemakers known as the herpesviruses. In addition to causing infectious mononucleosis, the Epstein-Barr virus also plays an important role in the development of two rare forms of human cancer, the first kind found exclusively among natives of West Africa and the other occurring in China.

Another group of troublemakers in the herpesvirus family are the herpes simplex viruses, or HSVs. HSV_1 causes irritating and unsightly cold sores around the lips, while its cousin, HSV_2, is responsible for genital herpes, a painful and recurring infection of the genital organs.

Some herpesviruses have a particularly unpleasant characteristic. They are very skillful at evading our immune defenses and "hiding out" in the body, so that once infected, we have great difficulty getting rid of them. A good example of this is the herpes zoster virus, responsible in childhood for ordinary chicken pox. This childhood disease clears up very quickly, but the zoster virus is not thrown off by our immune defenses as other viruses are. Rather, it sneaks into nerve cells in the spinal cord and remains quietly in hiding

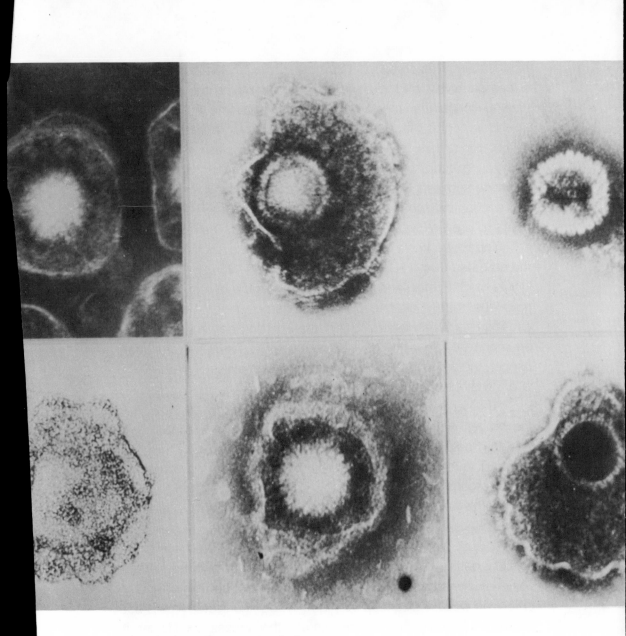

*An electronmicrograph of six
different herpes simplex viruses*

for many years. Decades later it may be reactivated—no one quite knows why—and cause a painful skin infection known as herpes zoster, or "shingles."

POLIO AND OTHER KILLERS

One of the most deadly of all viral infections is paralytic poliomyelitis, which used to strike down thousands of young people in the United States each year, killing many and permanently crippling many more, before a protective vaccine was discovered. Although, as mentioned earlier, it is basically an intestinal virus, the polio virus will sometimes migrate to the spinal cord and destroy the nerve cells there that control muscular motion all over the body. Partial or complete paralysis can result, and once the nerve cells are dead, the muscles can never recover their function. In what is called bulbar polio, nerve cells in the spinal cord or the brain are permanently destroyed, knocking out the muscles necessary for swallowing and even breathing and leading to an extremely high death rate.

Thanks to the widespread use of vaccines, polio in the United States is now uncommon, but it is by no means wiped out. It is merely held at bay, ever ready to strike unprotected individuals. All babies and children should have full, up-to-date immunization, and any adult under the age of forty should make sure his or her immunization was completed. More than anyone else, it is young adults who are hardest hit when polio strikes.

A few other viral diseases, once deadly killers, have also been controlled, thanks to worldwide vaccination programs and public-health measures. Yellow fever, once a widespread epidemic disease, is now seldom seen in humans, although the virus still causes sporadic epidemics among tropical monkeys. As for smallpox, the last reported case in the entire world occurred in 1977, and many health officials now believe the disease may at last have been permanently stamped out—the first infectious killer in all history to have been eradicated thanks to a deliberate effort on the part of humans.

Still other viral diseases are particularly notable because of certain unique characteristics. In mumps, a commonplace children's disease, the virus attacks cells in the salivary glands, causing a painful swelling of the cheeks and under the chin. The infection is relatively harmless in small children, but in teenagers or young adults the virus may also attack cells in the testicles of the male or the ovaries of the female and—especially in the male—may cause permanent sterility. Because of this threat, and because of the rare complications that can occur in young children, exposed youngsters may be protected with injections of mumps immune serum taken from people who have recovered from the disease or by inoculation with a longer-acting vaccine. Because the rubeola virus causing red measles is known to cause in some victims a dangerous encephalitis, or "brain fever," or other complications, doctors today recommend that all children be vaccinated against measles by the time they are ready to enter school. Vaccination against rubella is also recommended, particularly in girls before they reach childbearing age, because of serious malformations the rubella virus can cause in a developing baby if a mother-to-be contracts the disease during the first half of her pregnancy.

Modern scientists are still discovering new and unexpected kinds of viral diseases. In 1957, for example, American virologist Carleton Gajdusek began studying a strange form of brain deterioration known as *kuru*—"the shivering disease"—afflicting certain native tribes in New Guinea. After eight years of work, Gajdusek finally isolated the cause—one of the tiniest viruses ever discovered. This strange virus would live in the victim's body for years, successfully hiding from natural immune defenses and slowly destroying brain cells, one by one, all the while. Similar "slow viruses" have now been found to cause several other kinds of brain and nervous system disease.

TREATMENT OF
VIRAL INFECTIONS

Clearly, viral infections can run the entire spectrum, from the most minor to the most grave. But what can be done to treat them once they occur? Recently, a few antiviral drugs have been discovered that help to slow or prevent certain kinds of viral infection. A drug called amantadine, for example, seems to be able to block certain influenza infections, and adenine arabinoside, or ara-A, has been used since 1978 to combat some herpesvirus infections. For the most part, however, viruses are not affected by the kinds of antibiotics that stop bacterial infections so swiftly. For the vast majority of viral infections, the best treatment we know is still adequate rest, a nourishing diet, and patience enough to wait for the body's own natural defenses to come to the rescue. While waiting, simple medicines can sometimes alleviate the more uncomfortable symptoms— aspirin for headaches and aching muscles (although aspirin is no longer recommended for influenzas or chicken pox); nose drops and cough syrups for upper respiratory symptoms; and antinausea and antidiarrhea medicines for gastrointestinal symptoms.

In the long run, however, we must rely on the body's built-in capacity to resist and fight off the more minor viral invaders, and protect ourselves with vaccines, when possible, against the more dangerous viruses. The story of how those vaccines were first developed and how they work to prevent viral infection makes one of the most exciting chapters in the history of medical discovery, a chapter that is not yet closed even today.

●35

VACCINES AND IMMUNITY

From the very beginning of virus research, medical scientists faced a perplexing question. Obviously, viruses were capable of producing many severe, even fatal, infections in humans. Equally obvious, there was no way to cure viral infections after they started. But if there were no defenses against these dangerous infections, why had they not wiped people out of existence many centuries ago?

Today the answer seems simple. Some very effective defenses against viral infections do indeed exist—not external defenses involving miracle drugs or medical treatments, but *internal* defenses that help the virus victim fight off the infection. If the patient manages to survive long enough, his or her body alone will sooner or later fight off most viral invasions. The truly deadly viruses—rabies, yellow fever, smallpox, and the like—were those that killed quickly, before natural defenses could be adequately rallied. But for those who did survive, internal protection against future infections of the same disease seemed to linger on long after the virus was conquered, rendering the victim *immune* (from a Latin word meaning "exempt") from later infection by the same virus.

What was the nature of this natural defense mechanism against viral infections? How, exactly, did it work? Could weak defenses be strengthened, or speeded up? Could immunity be artificially stimulated against all kinds of viral infections, just as it had been against smallpox and rabies back in the days before viruses were even discovered? These are questions that virologists have been asking themselves since the earliest days of virus research; and in recent years some very encouraging answers have appeared.

ANTIGENS AND ANTIBODIES

Today we know our natural defenses against viruses depend upon a curious and complicated biochemical reaction that occurs within our bodies whenever viruses gain entrance. This is the so-called antigen-antibody reaction. In simple terms this means that whenever a strange, or "foreign," substance gains entrance to the body— especially a foreign protein—the body senses that it does not belong there and begins a complex internal chemical reaction to get rid of it, or at least to block it from further contact with the body's cells and tissues. Mere external contact with such a substance does not normally set this machinery in motion; we are constantly touching foreign substances, even eating for nourishment a wide variety of protein materials, without harmful effect. But let even a tiny bit of foreign protein—a pollen grain, for instance, or a protein-coated virus particle—get into the tissues under the skin, or work its way through the mucous membrane of the lungs or the intestines into the interior of the body, and a widespread reaction begins.

First, special patrolling cells called lymphocytes, wandering throughout all the tissues of the body, come in contact with the invading foreign protein (or antigen, to use the technical term). These lymphocytes recognize the protein as foreign, or "not-self" (that is, a substance that doesn't belong in the body), and, in effect, "take its measurements." The lymphocytes then become transformed into plasma cells, which respond to the presence of the foreign protein by manufacturing complex protein entities known as antibodies and dumping them into the bloodstream. These antibodies then flock to the place where the foreign protein has entered and work to destroy it or neutralize it.

We know that each antibody is "form-fitted" to its particular antigen so perfectly that it is capable of immobilizing that specific antigen and no other. As early as 1885 the great German chemist and physician Paul Ehrlich speculated that each antibody might be specially shaped to fit around its corresponding antigen the way a lock fits around a key, and thus prevent it from reacting with any other substance. Although not entirely accurate, this "lock and key" picture is still a close approximation of what actually happens. We now know that invading viruses must attach themselves to the walls of susceptible cells in order to invade them. Antibodies, which are composed of protein material, seem able to clamp onto the protein shells of the virus particles and thus prevent them from attaching themselves to the cell walls in the first place. The virus particles are then held helpless prisoners until white blood cells known as phagocytes arrive at the scene to absorb and destroy them.

Unfortunately, an effective antigen-antibody reaction takes time to get started after a viral invasion. This means that viral infections can often become well entrenched before sufficient opposing antibodies can be manufactured. And the antibodies can do nothing about the viruses that have already invaded the victim's cells. All they can do is help immobilize and destroy the new virus particles being produced and released from the already infected cells.

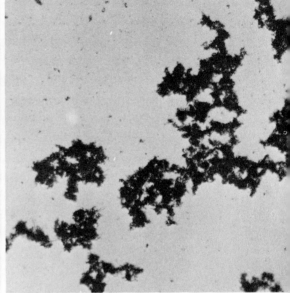

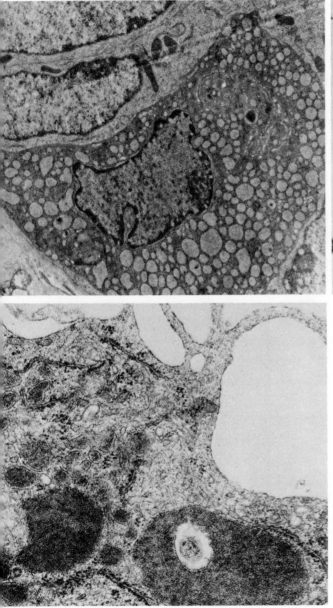

When foreign proteins enter our bodies, plasma cells (above left) respond by producing antibodies (above right), which attach themselves to these particles and inhibit their action. Later, white blood cells known as phagocytes (left) arrive and literally "eat" the invaders.

But if the initial wave of infection is not too severe, or if the cells already damaged are not vital to life, sufficient numbers of antibodies are eventually formed to neutralize all the new virus particles being formed, and the victim gradually recovers from the infection. What is more, these antibodies continue to be manufactured in the body, months or even years after the viral infection is over, ready to swing into action instantly any time that particular virus attempts another invasion. Thus, as a result of the first infection, the victim may remain immune to reinfection from the same virus source for years, sometimes even a lifetime.

THE SEARCH FOR VACCINES

Doctors speak of the immunity that arises from an actual previous infection as "active immunity." Because it may last for a very long time, this is the best possible protection from recurrence of the infection in question—as long as the victim manages to survive the first attack! But is there no way to artificially stimulate immunity without having to subject the patient to the dangers of the disease itself?

In fact, there is a way. One person's immunity can sometimes be passed on to others simply by passing on some of the immune person's antibodies to a susceptible patient. This is, in fact, the basis of a natural mechanism that protects infants from certain viral infections in their first few months of life. If the expectant mother has had measles sometime earlier in her life, some of the mother's antibodies against the measles virus will cross into the baby's bloodstream while she is carrying the fetus, so that the newborn baby will be immune to measles for some months after birth.

Doctors speak of this as an "acquired immunity." It can work in other ways, too. If someone susceptible to mumps is given inoculations of blood serum from someone who has recently recovered from a mumps infection, the susceptible person will develop an acquired immunity for a brief period of time. The main trouble with such acquired immunity is that it doesn't last very long; the acquired antibodies will soon disappear from the recipient's bloodstream, leaving him or her vulnerable again within a few weeks or months.

This does not mean that acquired immunity is useless. It protects many newborn infants from diseases such as measles or whooping cough until their bodies have grown strong enough to see them through. And if a person is exposed to a dangerous viral infection like hepatitis A, even a brief immunity acquired from gamma globulin injections can be a lifesaver. But for many of the viral diseases, a long-lasting active immunity would be far more preferable. The big question facing early virologists was how to induce active immunity without subjecting the patient to the dangers of the full-blown infection.

One way was suggested by Edward Jenner's successful smallpox vaccination experiments back in the 1790s. Jenner didn't know *why* his patients became immune to the dreaded smallpox just by subjecting them to a mild case of cowpox; it was enough that it worked. Today we know why. Although the live vaccinia virus of cowpox causes only a mild localized infection compared to the ravages of the smallpox virus, the two viruses themselves are so very similar that the body's antibody factory cannot tell them apart. The antibodies formed in response to the cowpox virus blocked the more virulent smallpox virus as well. We also know now that this is one of the extremely rare exceptions to the rule that any given antibody will block just one specific antigen and no other. The success of Jenner's vaccination technique was, in fact, a stroke of fantastic good luck.

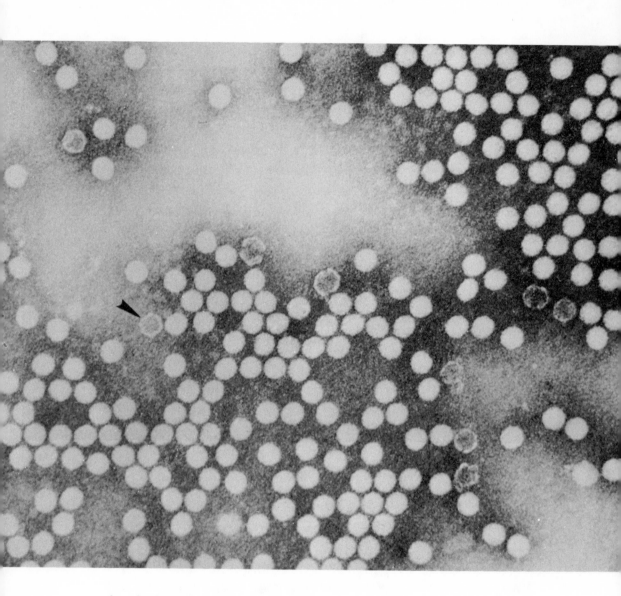

An electronmicrograph of the polio virus.
This type of virus was used by Dr. Jonas Salk
in his work with "killed-virus" vaccines.

Yet the basic principle, once it was understood, was exceedingly important. Introducing a living virus into the human body, in one form or another, could stimulate the production of protective antibodies, leading to lasting active immunity. If this could be done without risking dangerous illness from the invading virus, successful vaccines might be made.

But how? Most researchers were convinced that it was the nucleic acid packet at the core of the virus that was the infective part, but perhaps it was the protein coating that triggered the formation of antibodies. If this were so, then destroying the virus' core before it was used for injection as a vaccine might strip it of its power to cause infection, yet still preserve its antibody-stimulating protein. The person inoculated with such a vaccine should be safe from infection but at the same time might develop a long-lasting active immunity.

It seemed to be a long shot, but it worked. A familiar example of a successful "killed virus" vaccine was the one developed by Dr. Jonas Salk and his team at the University of Pittsburgh in 1953 and put into use in 1955 against the three major strains of polio viruses. Salk killed the virulent viruses with formaldehyde before injecting them as a vaccine. Just as he hoped, their protein shells triggered the formation of antipolio antibodies. Those who were vaccinated with this "killed virus" vaccine developed active immunity to polio for the first time.

Unfortunately, there were some problems with the Salk vaccine. Four separate shots were required to build immunity up to a lasting peak. Perhaps more serious, antibodies formed against the injected vaccine did not adequately block the reproduction of polio viruses in the intestinal tract—which was, after all, their natural habitat—so that the spread of the wild virus was not completely controlled.

Thus a different approach to creating a polio vaccine was considered. Rather than killing the viruses, researchers tried weakening them severely by passing them repeatedly through animal or egg cultures. After many such passages the viruses, although still very much alive, had been attenuated to the point that they could not cause dangerous disease. In 1955, Dr. Albert Sabin of the University of Cincinnati College of Medicine began testing a polio vaccine he had made of such live but attenuated viruses.

This vaccine had the additional advantage that it could be taken orally, rather than having to be injected into the bloodstream, and could produce immunity to polio viruses in the intestine as well as in the bloodstream. The Sabin vaccine was first approved for use in the United States in 1961, and, along with the Salk vaccine is still in use today.

Yet another means was used to guard against possible side effects of a vaccine made from live, attenuated viruses when the earliest vaccine against rubeola (red measles) was developed. We might not think of measles as a terribly dangerous disease, but every year a certain number of victims are permanently crippled or even killed by complications such as measles encephalitis—an inflammation of the brain caused by the virus—or pneumonia caused by bacteria attacking the lungs of the virus-weakened victim. Unfortunately, when the first measles vaccine was made from live, inactivated rubeola viruses, the vaccine itself caused moderately severe measles, with complications appearing in rare cases. To prevent this, an injection of gamma globulin was given along with the vaccine. The gamma globulin successfully suppressed any measles symptoms arising from the vaccine itself until the body had enough time to build its own permanent antirubeola antibodies. Modern measles vaccines, made from more severely weakened viruses, cause only a day or so of mild fever, with no severe measles symptoms

44•

Dr. Albert Sabin tried a different approach to combating polio. Rather than using dead viral material, he made a vaccine of live, but weakened, polio viruses.

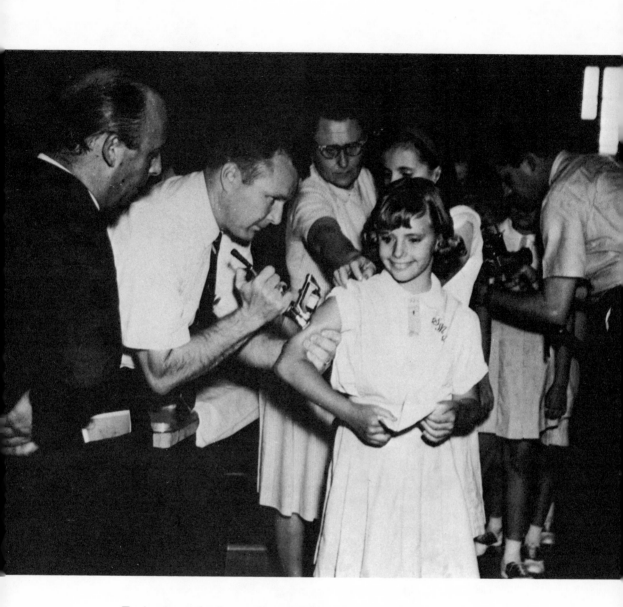

Today, vaccinations are routinely administered to help prevent a variety of viral diseases. Here a doctor uses a jet injector at an immunization clinic.

and no complications, so that gamma globulin is no longer given with the vaccine. With widespread use of the measles vaccine, fewer than two thousand cases of measles occurred in the United States in 1981, and health officials expect the country to be free of this disease (except for cases brought into the country from outside) by the mid-1980s, making it the second serious viral disease to be virtually eradicated.

Vaccine research continues even today. Recently, for example, scientists at the University of California at San Francisco finally perfected a vaccine against hepatitis B—even though no way could be found to grow the virus itself in the laboratory. The vaccine was made not from the virus proper, but from a special surface protein surrounding the virus core, which could act as an antibody-stimulating antigen. At first, this surface protein could be obtained only by slow, extremely costly extraction from the blood of people carrying the disease. But using the new techniques of genetic engineering, the California researchers found a way to cause a simple strain of intestinal bacteria to produce large quantities of the necessary surface protein safely and inexpensively in the laboratory. As mentioned earlier, the new hepatitis B vaccine was approved by the FDA in 1981 and is now available to protect people with high risk of contracting hepatitis B.

Important as vaccine research may be, it is by no means the only direction that modern virus research has taken. New and exciting work is being done today to study the basic biochemical nature of viruses, the many effects they can have on living creatures, and the long-term roles they may play in such vital areas as the development of cancer, the phenomenon of aging, and, indeed, the alterations they may make in the basic genetic nature of our cells. The story of viruses is not complete without a chapter, which is still being written today, on current virus research.

MODERN VIRUS RESEARCH

Early virus researchers had one major and overriding goal—to find ways to cure, control, or prevent dangerous viral diseases. In the last thirty years great strides have been made toward this goal. Although specific cures have yet to be found, many of the most deadly viral diseases can be prevented and epidemics controlled by vaccination. In addition to smallpox, yellow fever, and poliomyelitis, the list of preventable viral diseases now includes rubeola, rubella, mumps, many strains of influenza, and hepatitis B. At the same time, scientists are searching for drugs or other agents to stop, or at least modify, many other viral diseases. Among the most interesting of these "other agents" is a naturally occurring substance known as human interferon.

A NATURAL VIRUS-KILLER

In 1957, a Scottish virologist, Alick Isaacs, and a Swiss microbiologist, Jean Lindenmann, discovered a natural protein substance in the bloodstream that seemed to interfere with the reproduction of viruses in infected cells and thus effectively block the development of viral infection. The substance, called interferon, was produced by white blood cells in people whose bodies had been stimulated by a virus invasion. Later it was found that another form of interferon was produced by certain kinds of fibrous tissue cells.

At first it was hoped that interferon might be used as a medicine to combat a wide variety of viral infections. And indeed, when the tiny amounts available were tested against cold viruses, for instance, the substance seemed quite effective in preventing colds. Unfortunately, it was formed in such very tiny amounts, and was so very difficult to extract from human blood, that it was far too costly for use as a medicine.

Although interferon research continued in various European countries in the 1960s and early 1970s, interest in it in the United States did not really pick up until the late 1970s, when it was found to slow the growth of certain kinds of cancer in laboratory animals. This fit in with a widespread suspicion that certain viruses might have a role in triggering the wild, uncontrolled growth that occurs in cancer cells. In 1978, the American Cancer Society launched the largest test so far in the use of interferon to treat cancer in humans, and researchers have been able to use genetic-engineering techniques to produce human interferon quite cheaply from yeast cultures in the laboratory. So far, it is too early to evaluate the effectiveness of interferon in combating cancer, but such studies have brought the old question of a virus-cancer connection into very sharp focus.

VIRUSES AND CANCER

Once scientists had discovered that viruses were really not much more than tiny, encapsulated bits of hereditary material very similar

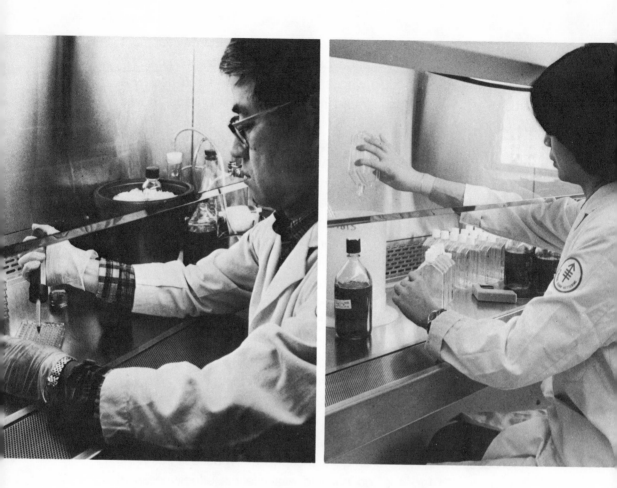

*Left: interferon, a natural protein that seems to slow
down the reproduction of viruses, may prove helpful
in controlling or curing cancer. Here a technician
is adding interferon to cells infected by a virus.
Right: today, using genetic-engineering techniques,
interferon can be produced efficiently in the laboratory.
In this photograph, cells are being treated with
cultures to prepare them for interferon production.*

to the hereditary material found in all living cells and capable of causing permanent and inheritable changes in the cells of their hosts, they realized that they had within their grasp a possible means for studying the hereditary patterns of normal and abnormal cells alike—perhaps even including the abnormal cells found in cancer.

The idea that viruses might be involved in the development of cancer has been around for almost as long as viruses themselves have been known. As early as 1908, Danish researchers Wilhelm Ellerman and Olaf Bang had shown that certain animal viruses could cause a form of leukemia in chickens, although nobody knew how or why. In 1911, American physician Francis Peyton Rous developed a clear filtrate from certain tumors in chickens that could produce new tumors in healthy chickens. For a while there was a flurry of activity to try to identify viruses with cancers in higher animals and humans, all to no avail, and by the time the first really suggestive evidence of a true virus-cancer link began to appear in the early 1930s, nobody was much interested any more.

Why this lack of interest? For one thing, a number of other factors far removed from viruses had been implicated in various human cancers. Excessive exposure to X rays or other kinds of radiation, for example, was clearly linked to cancer. So was exposure to certain so-called carcinogenic, or "cancer-causing," chemicals such as coal-tar derivatives and various synthetic dyes. On the other hand, there was not even a single instance of any virus cultured and identified from human cancer tissue. Unfortunately, those early workers did not know enough about viruses to realize that a virus-induced change within a cell might be passed on from generation to generation, perhaps leading to cancerous changes sometime later, even after the virus that had caused the change in the first place was no longer present—at least not in the form of a recognizable virus. But as new knowledge about the nature and behavior of viruses piled up, more and more researchers began to reconsider the whole question.

As we have seen, every virus is made up of two parts: an outer shell, composed of protein molecules, and an inner core, made up of nucleic acid, in the form of either DNA or RNA. What is more, viral DNA and RNA have been found to be exceedingly similar to the DNA and RNA found in the nucleus of all living cells. In the cell nucleus this hereditary material is concentrated in thousands of little packets known as genes, strung together like beads on a thread to form chromosomes.

THE "MASTER MOLECULES"

It is the DNA in these genes, and their particular location on a chromosome, that determines the characteristics of the daughter cells when the parent cells reproduce by cell division. If, for some reason, a gene or group of genes has broken off from its chromosome, or has become displaced from its normal location before cell division occurs, the daughter cells may be markedly different from the parent cell, and these differences will be passed on to the next generation of cells, and the next, and the next, and so on.

But the DNA and RNA in living cells control far more than the heredity of those cells. They act as "master molecules," controlling virtually every aspect of the cell's structure and behavior. Some genes direct the manufacture of proteins and enzymes within the cell. Others monitor the energy-producing reactions that occur within the cell. And, very significantly, still others control how fast the cell will grow and reproduce, and in what kind of tissue the cell can grow.

Ordinarily, cell reproduction is a very orderly matter. Except during periods of accelerated body growth or sudden maturation (such as during infancy or adolescence, for example), new cells are normally produced only when needed to replace old, worn-out cells. What is more, cells making up one kind of tissue will ordinarily grow only in that kind of tissue and no other. Bone cells grow in bone, muscle cells in muscle, and so forth. But if something happens to alter the orderly gene control of cell growth, certain cells may begin to reproduce rapidly and wildly, regardless of need and totally out of control. Even worse, the special characteristics that distinguish a cell of bone tissue, muscle tissue, or glandular tissue may be lost, so that a cell that originally would grow only in its own kind of tissue begins to invade surrounding tissues. Control of cell growth may be so completely disrupted that these sick, abnormal cells break loose from their neighbors and float around in the bloodstream or in lymph channels, later to lodge in distant places and develop new clusters of sick, wildly growing cells. It is precisely this type of wild and invasive cell growth that we know as cancer.

With this picture in mind, we can see why scientists today are fairly certain that some kind of virus-cancer connection exists, at least in some forms of cancer. The DNA or RNA in a virus, acting much like the DNA or RNA in the living cells it invades, can take over the cell's protein-making mechanism and force the cell to manufacture nothing but viral DNA or RNA. The virus' control may be so complete that in a matter of minutes from the time it invades the cell, the cell has been totally exhausted building new virus particles and finally bursts apart, scattering hundreds of new viruses abroad to infect more cells.

But certain viruses behave differently. They may simply attach their DNA or RNA to that already present in the cell nucleus and then sit and wait. No new viruses are formed. Indeed, all traces of the invading virus may vanish except for that fragment of viral DNA or RNA tacked onto the cell's hereditary material. But when that cell

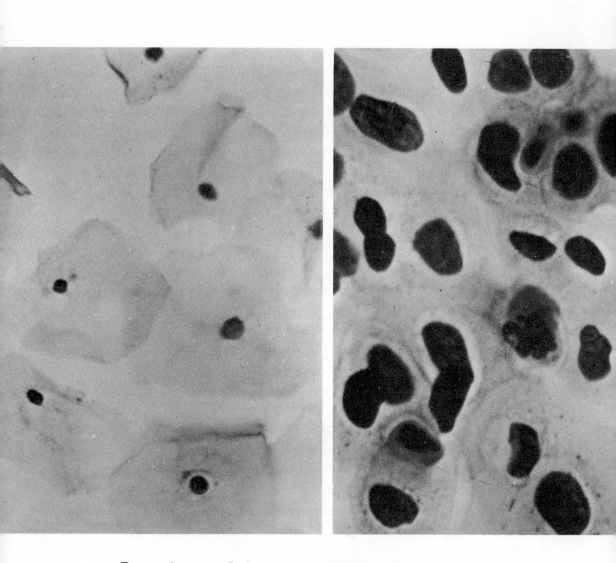

Researchers are finding growing evidence of a
virus-cancer connection. Normal cervix cells (left)
may be invaded by viruses, which take over the
reproductive mechanism of the cells and cause the
abnormal growth that is known as cancer (right).

reproduces itself, it reproduces the viral DNA fragment right along with its own. In effect, the virus has silently altered the cell's hereditary mechanism. Some new messages have been added to the cell's genetic code, and these new messages are passed on from one generation of the cell to the next.

In many cases the end result is simply that the cell proceeds merrily on its way until something triggers the viral DNA or RNA to take over the cell's life functions and start producing more virus particles. But those virus genes attached to the cell's chromosomes might have an even more profound effect on the cell. The "hidden" virus genes might so completely alter the cell, for example, that its normal, orderly growth and reproductive pattern is broken down, transforming it into a cancer cell that begins dividing wildly, totally out of control.

Scientists today believe that this may be at least one of the ways in which cancers can arise in lower animals, and possibly in humans as well. There need be no identifiable living virus present in cancer tissue in order for this to be so; all that would be needed would be altered hereditary material in the cancerous cells. Nor would such a change from normal cell growth to cancerous growth necessarily have to begin immediately. The altered cells might well remain quiescent for years, maybe even decades, until some outside influence came along—exposure to excessive radiation, for example, or contact with a carcinogenic chemical—to trigger the outburst of wild growth. It may be, in fact, that a whole succession or "cascade" of events must occur for a cancer to develop, with the virus playing just one part in the whole series of events.

Whatever the details may be, virus researchers are hard at work studying how such a virus-cancer connection might operate in humans. Some are learning more about the basic nature and behavior of viruses in general. In 1965, Dr. S. Spiegelmann produced a

•55

synthetic (artificial) RNA molecule in his laboratory that had the power to infect living cells. In effect, he had produced an artificial virus! Two years later, in 1967, Drs. A. Kornberg, N. Goulian, and R. L. Sinsheimer went a step further and put together synthetic viral DNA. This substance could not only infect living cells but could also take over control of the cells' biochemical function, just as natural viruses do. When the infected cells finally burst apart, they released huge quantities of newly made viral DNA, demonstrating once again the power of DNA to bring about its own replication once it got inside a living cell.

Others have been studying a possible virus-cancer connection more directly. Led by research teams at such major research centers as the National Cancer Institute in Bethesda, Maryland, and the Memorial Sloan-Kettering Institute in New York, scientists in medical centers all over the world are searching for definite proof that certain human cancers are inextricably connected with viruses. So far, few answers are in, but if viruses do have a role in the development of cancer and that role can finally be identified and clearly understood, it could be a happy day for the future of human health. As American physician and virologist Dr. Robert Huebner recently expressed it, "If it is a virus, we can handle it. We can find a way to control, perhaps to prevent cancer."

VIRUSES AND
THE SECRET OF LIFE

How soon can we expect definite answers to emerge? No one yet can say, but with all the suggestive evidence that has piled up during recent years, we may not have long to wait. Some researchers hope a breakthrough will come within the next decade.

Meanwhile, other researchers are using viruses as tools to study the life processes of living cells. In the chromosomes of complex cells, DNA molecules may contain thousands upon thousands of genes; determining which specific gene performs which life function in a cell can be an impossible task. But viral DNA may contain as few as a dozen genes, making their individual functions much easier to trace. What is more, we have seen that many viruses tend to undergo mutations due to spontaneous changes in their gene arrangements. By studying the variation in function brought about by these gene changes, still more can be learned about the life-controlling power of individual genes. With viral DNA to work with, virologists are slowly but surely stripping the enigmatic viruses of their mysteries, finding ways to take their "master molecules" apart and put them back together again, and observing the changes that come about as a result of these manipulations. Some scientists believe that the secret of life itself may lie in these "master molecules"—that their function may spell the difference between a living, reproducing cell on the one hand and an inert puddle of fluids and chemicals on the other. It would be ironic indeed if the lowly viruses, so long considered an implacable foe of humankind, should ultimately provide us with the key to the secret of life itself!

Viruses have been among us, playing their deadly role in human affairs, for as long as people have walked the earth. But now, perhaps, they are destined to play a different role.

GLOSSARY

Acquired immunity—a temporary immunity that arises when protective antibodies from an immune person are transferred to another person, either from mother to baby or by inoculation.

Active immunity—an immunity that arises from an actual previous bacterial or viral infection, or through vaccination.

Antibodies—special substances formed by our bodies to help fight off foreign invaders such as viruses.

Attenuation—an intentional weakening of a virulent virus in the laboratory, or rendering it less infective, for purposes of producing a protective vaccine.

Bacteria—one-celled plantlike organisms that in some cases can cause infections.

Cell—the smallest self-contained unit of life. Our bodies are made up of billions of living cells grouped together to form organs and body tissues.

Chromosomes—long, narrow, dark-staining structures within the cell nucleus that contain the cell's hereditary material (DNA and RNA) formed into strings of tiny bundles called genes.

DNA—deoxyribonucleic acid. A complex substance usually found in the nuclei of cells, molecules of which make up the hereditary material of the cell and pass it on from one generation of cells to the next. (*See also* nucleic acids.)

Genetic engineering—the generic term for various modern laboratory techniques that involve manipulating DNA or RNA in bacterial cells to produce desired protein products such as interferons, hepatitis B vaccine, and so forth.

Immunity—the condition of being protected against (i.e., *immune to*) a specific infection because the body's immune defense system has been stimulated.

Inoculation—injection (or oral administration) of a vaccine into the body.

Interferons—special protein substances naturally manufactured in tiny quantities by white blood cells and other tissues to interfere with the growth of invading viruses.

Lymphocytes—small, free-moving cells with large nuclei. Lymphocytes are manufactured in the bone marrow and make up one class of white blood cells. They play many important roles in the body's immune defense system.

Mutation—an inheritable change in a cell or virus. Some mutations occur spontaneously (i.e., for no known reason); others may be caused by known outside influences such as radiation.

Nucleic acids—several types of complex chemicals occurring in all living cells, especially as a component of cell-nucleus protein and in the cores of virus particles. The nucleic acids DNA and RNA carry the special genetic codes of the cells or viruses. (*See also* DNA *and* RNA.)

Phagocytes—various forms of white blood cells capable of engulfing and digesting invading bacteria, virus particles, and so forth.

Plasma cells—cells in the bone marrow, derived from lymphocytes, that manufacture antibodies.

Proteins—large, nitrogen-containing organic compounds that form the major building blocks of cells and tissues in all living organisms.

RNA—ribonucleic acid. A complex substance usually found in the nuclei or cytoplasm of cells, often responsible for the manufacture of various vital proteins. (*See also* nucleic acid.)

Vaccination—inoculation of a person with a modified virus, bacterial protein, or some other substance to stimulate an immune response.

Virology—the study of the nature and behavior of viruses.

Viruses—tiny microorganisms, generally much smaller than bacteria and composed of DNA or RNA within a protein envelope. Viruses can invade body cells and cause viral infections.

ADDITIONAL READING

Asimov, Isaac. *Asimov's Guide to Science* (pp. 653–684). New York: Basic Books, 1972.

Brooks, Stewart M. *The World of the Viruses*. New York: A. S. Barnes, 1970.

Eron, Carol. *The Virus That Ate Cannibals*. New York: Macmillan, 1981.

Fuller, John G. *Fever! The Hunt for a New Killer Virus*. New York: Reader's Digest Press/E. P. Dutton, 1974.

Nourse, Alan E. *Your Immune System*. New York: Franklin Watts, 1982.

Sigel, M. Michael, and Ann R. Beasley. *Viruses, Cells and Hosts*. New York: Holt, Rinehart & Winston, 1965.

INDEX

Respiratory infections, 25
    treatment of, 35
Rhinoviruses, 25–26
Rickettsia, 7, 16
RNA (ribonucleic acid), 11–12, 52–53,
    56
        synthetic (artificial), 56
Rocky Mountain spotted fever, 7
Rous, Francis Peyton, 51
Rubella (German measles), 6, 29, 34,
    48
Rubeola (red measles), 5–6, 29, 34,
    44, 48
        vaccine against, 44, 47

Sabin, Albert, 15, 23, 44, *45*
Salk, Jonas, 15, *42*, 43–44
Scarlet fever, 7
"Shingles," 33
"Shivering disease," 34
Sinsheimer, R. L., 56
Smallpox, 1–2, *3*, 6, 16, 33–34, 36–37,
    41, 48
Spiegelmann, S., 55
Stanley, Wendell M., 18
Syphilis, 6

T2 virus, 18
Tobacco mosaic virus, 16–18, 20
Tuberculosis, 7
Typhus fever, 7

Vaccination, 1–2, 33, 41, *46*, 48

Vaccines, 23–24, 30, 33–35, 43–44,
    45, 47
Vaccinia virus, *3*, 18, *19*, 41
Viral infections
    body's natural defenses against,
        14, 28, 30–31, 35–38, 40–41,
        43
    symptoms of, 29, 31
    treatment of, 29, 31, 33–35, 48.
        See also Vaccines
Virology and virologists, 9, 15, 17–18,
    24, 31, 34, 37, 41, 48, 55–57
Virus-cancer connection, 49, 51, 53,
    54, 55–56
Viruses
    behavior of, 12, 14, 23, 26, 38,
        40, 53, 63
    compared to bacteria, 7, 9–11,
        20, 28
    destruction of, 10
    and heredity, 51–52, 55
    mutations of, 23–24, 57
    nature of, 5, 7, 9–11, 14, 17–20,
        47, 49, 53
    "secret of life" of, 11
    synthetic, 23
    transmission of, 9, 26, 30–31

White blood cells. *See* Phagocytes
Whooping cough, 41
Woodruff, Alice M., 23

Yellow fever, 6, 16–17, 33, 36, 48

ABOUT
THE AUTHOR

Alan E. Nourse is a former practicing physician and a distinguished science writer for children and adults. For Franklin Watts, he has authored many popular First Books in the health area, including *Menstruation: Just Plain Talk; Fractures, Dislocations, and Sprains;* and the just-published *Your Immune System.*

    Dr. Nourse, who lives in the state of Washington, is also an astronomy buff and recently revised his First Book of *The Giant Planets* for Watts, to include many of the new discoveries of the *Voyager* missions.